A CARAVAN OF POETRY

STEVE WHITMILL

authorHOUSE®

AuthorHouse™ UK
1663 Liberty Drive
Bloomington, IN 47403 USA
www.authorhouse.co.uk
Phone: UK TFN: 0800 0148641 (Toll Free inside the UK)
        UK Local: 02036 956322 (+44 20 3695
        6322 from outside the UK)

Published by AuthorHouse 07/26/2021

ISBN: 978-1-6655-9173-7 (sc)
ISBN: 978-1-6655-9172-0 (e)

Print information available on the last page.

Acknowledgements

I would like to thank my wife, Michelle, for enabling me the space and time to work on this poetry and my friend Lawrence Butterfield for giving me hope.

Dedication

These words are dedicated to my son, Zak, without whom I would have no light in my life.

Contents

102

Where are you going, you and your son?
I am over here – me and my little 'uns
As you pant by, puffing and wobbling…
I don't know if you're going far, but I think
It would be easier by car

Why are you straining yourselves?
Are you getting any thinner?
I thought life was mostly about eating grass and ending up
as someone's dinner

You think us sheep are stupid…
Going 'BAAA' and emitting dung…
Let me tell you a secret: this morning I was thinking about
Kant and Jung.
We speak Latin, too, you know and devour Dickens and
more….
Although we don't care much for the Apocalypse and 1984

But Low! You are back again!
By the time you have passed, there will be no trace on my
brain
Until some other woolly human being comes this way again

Yet I know you love your boy, as I do mine
As love crosses boundaries, with men and sheep immortal
over time

I have a name (you know) but that's not for you!
I hear you call 'Zak' – is that what you all are?
For us, I don't know – we all look the same from afar

So, its farewell, goodbye or adieu!
It's been fun seeing you
From your quizzical sheep number 102.

The Stealer

I didn't used to exist…
In the days when children had a childhood and when time was
Something to be filled with choice, creativity and fulfilment

I slowly grew, though, to dominate your life
In fact, to such an extent, that you cannot put me down –
you cannot function without me in your hand

I am The Stealer, who will rob you of your time and rob you of your privacy
I will stop you being yourself and diminish your personal social skills
I will claim you my psychological prisoner

You are my slave and I am your God
You are addicted to me as I sap the life blood out of you,
Every minute of every day
You are utterly in my control

My acolytes tell you what to do and my algorithms befuddle your mind
Pulling you into a world of instant gratification and shallow reward
I don't want you to process or organize your thinking. You don't need to

Who am I? – don't you know?

I am your phone

Dark Trees

Chimneys of wood reaching to the sky
Smooth, Ent-like with dendritic hair-do's
They too, huddled together in the terrible storm, clumped
tight and still amongst the wetness and turmoil, positioned
on those barren heights
I found them foreboding, as I ran into their midst: their
company: their kind
Ramrod tall with waving arms and varnish-less fingers

Yet, I thought I could hear them talk of the crying wind and
intruding rain
Dripping and penetrated, I looked around into this dark
world where light
was expelled and sound trapped.
My head turned at every creak and crack as I half-expected
them to move against me
Frightened to touch and careful not to walk, I stood without
motion: breath held, fists clenched and
with chest heaving I stared into their depths – their
impenetrable interior…their soul

The fear of the dark unknown pushed me back onto the
borders of these beings, where the wildness pushed and
washed at their extremities
I ran and dare not look back – the fear of their amassed
power panicked me and I gave myself up
back into the morass of the outside elements: at least there,
I knew who my enemy was
As I ran out, I swear I heard them cackle and laugh at me.
Once again, they had expelled the intruders that were axe-
wielders with their chainsaw-eyes.

The Pool

A dichotomy of lives, lives the lively pool
For pleasure, life and death are also within its soul
By daylight the waters invite and speak with the children
with cooing whiplash tones.
Such joy! such colours and fathomless enjoyment invite
the young multi-coloured, sparkling children.
They scream, scramble and succumb to the cooling,
soothing waters with
their images refracted and reflexes slowed in a different
world of hedonistic pleasure, that begs them
to meld with the medium

But when the covers are pulled over at night, and the sun
goes down the waters go quiet
They reflect on the happenings of the daytime – the fun, the
silliness and delights.
The flickering surfaces and turbulent depths are at rest, only
speaking to the circulated bubbles
that are pushed out by the vented mouthpiece
Warnings advise not to explore under this skin; not be daring
and seek what lies below...
For that is the pool's own world – not yours; where the hours
of quietness bely the regeneration of the waters and the
revitalisation of its voices

For now, the covers that control the waters reveal an almost
silent and almost lifeless pool, that is asleep.

Dead Caravans

Rows, sunken like fallen dominoes: the Stonehenge
monoliths of the caravan graveyard
Drunken, tilting and listless, they may be down and out – but
they somehow still
maintain their majesty and presence.
Six of the best and the worst: six with broken windows,
doors and wheels and six without any love
Holding on, up to their haunches in deep grass – in pain
and aged.
These old caravans are waiting to die

You can still see their glory if you look closely....
Peek through the dislodged windows and the inside is still
breathing but on life-support.
These once glorious holiday emporiums have a 'DNR' label
on them – they will not return to regain their former glory or
purpose.
The flapping curtains flail the sides and the doors slap back
and forth, dancing with the sides
Damp replaces warmth and stains cover the surfaces where
once games were played and meals were taken

But close your eyes and reimagine the laughs of children,
the circus of childhood and the respite
purpose of these caravans; burning August days and close
torpid nights, never cooling down with
rails draped with swimsuits and towels; watercraft fighting
for space on the decking.

Close your eyes and smell the barbeque and hear the clink-chink of wine glasses on a hot summer evening: you *must* be able to see a child's lost toy or teddy hiding under a chair or wedged down the side of a bed – mustn't you?

Ghosts are now the only spirits at home here, these days: they jaunt and haunt these greying, broken places....
But somewhere, you know, memories linger on and the families that loved *them* smile to themselves – photographs come out and suddenly the caravans are once again alive.

Love

If God is a concept, surely love is too
A battle between soul and body
A discourse between guilt and honesty
A fucking distress

Stupid and irrational
Threatening and deniable
Consuming and withering
It can fuck you up

Discard sensibility
Jettison morality
Ignore well-being
Be consumed into love

A body - an alternative
Something you cannot do without
It's you: it's her....
It's you both

It will never leave: it is so strong. It is undeniable.
You want to fuck her and she wants to fuck you
What can you do?
I am in pieces

June 2021
Dedicated to Grace

Looking Outside

She looks through the swaying net curtains
and registers the shouts and happiness of the holidaymakers passing by
The hot June sun does not warm her brow nor tan her thin white legs
The confinement that is her life, the estrangement from all childhood pleasures, no longer bring tears to her wan and pallid face
Her life is forever crashed like the waves on the nearby rocks: her hopes and aspirations played out
by the multi-coloured children on the beach

They don't know about her or her secluded existence
Their luck, their freedom and joys will not lighten the insurmountable burden of her cerebral palsy.
The love she has and the love she gets is unconditional – its intensity and dedication never ending
But it is not love grown through edging adolescence or from the ties of carefree childhood, but it is
draw from those who care and love her so deeply.

This child is in the palms of God: her beauty is the love she brings and gives, and her happiness comes from within her soul
The children on the beach and in the sea are the same as her, yet their worlds are shatteringly different.
Yet she yearns for the next holiday visit where the cries of children are the proxy of happiness to her.

Agent Orange

I know I'm pretty visible
But all the others don't see it at all – they don't know.
I'm here in secret, you see - I'm here to watch people – to
see things and report back
So, I'm not really a sheep at all….

The field stays the same: rain, grass and repetitious grazing
They are all the same: they all look the same, do the same
and are the same
But me? well, I'm different: I can read write, have read
classics, can use the internet – I just *look* like
a sheep

So, when the tourists stroll by; when they throw their rubbish
in the lane and deride the beauty of the countryside as
being boring and a nothing, I take note.
I can tell other people about them: I can dob them in.
I am definitely not like other sheep – my mark tells you that.

So just carry on: ignore me.
If it wasn't for the orange splash on my back, you wouldn't
even know I was different
But how wrong you would be: one message, one call and
you're history.
Your love of yourself and disregard of nature will unravel you.
So be aware: I'm watching you.

The Last Caravan

They put the oldest customers here....
They can't make the journey back to reception or the bus stop, you see
These caravans are coffins with net curtains
The rusted children's bikes are rusted to the rusted step rails and
Serve as a reminder of the industrial tourist age of caravans

They don't clean here often, either. Their little buggies have extra-range batteries and all-weather coverings but they still don't get this far....
The low paid women who suffer have hardy faces and bright waterproof overalls: they don't smile often and go about their work without complaining
The pathways are encroached with algae and moss – a return to nature and a rejection of mankind: the last caravans are a carbuncle in this area: all for sale, empty and unloved.

We unlock the door and pile in, dragging heavy bags full of clothes. It smells of old caravan with its solar stillness
The caravan shudders at the impact of small feet, as the fusty net curtains are swept back allowing the marshes beyond to peer in.
Dead flies lie on their backs – this mausoleum was too much even for them.
At night, the quiet seeps in to reclaim its space and the blackness and bleakness of our location consumes neighbouring vans.

In the morning we go to reception to seek out life. The girl behind the desk looks up at us oddly

'Oh, you found us then…. it's quite a way isn't it. Not many come this far'

I look at the location map on the wall and am sure our caravan should be in the sea: it's moving in that direction, I know it is

Upon return we resuscitate the caravan by turning on all the lights and the heating and for a while it is cryogenically unfrozen.

The Market

The cornucopia of the market agitates in the old quarter
And the collision of culture melds with the defence of old
territories and stakes.
Old animosities may be settled here today or inflamed
The buzz of trade and exchanges of friendship are kinetic and
pinch-points of disagreement shrill alongside laughter, deals
and bartering as the street hums to a
thousand touches of elbows and to the dead shuffling of
bank notes

The rivers of colours are broken by the old hunched traders
and the spangled tourists
who come with their Nikons swaying in the still hot air,
elevated by extreme perspiration
Odours compete for prominence with the rancid next to the
fresh: dead meat strung up, laughing,
while exotic fruits choke as they reach for sunlight and moisture
The cacophony of noise is deafening in the still street air,
while the flow of trade staggers like a drunk,
from side to side, while the dust rises constantly, kept down
by spit and urine.

But then, the day is over and they are all gone leaving the
detritus of trade and the evidence of human exertion
The thoroughfare withdraws into itself and is a shadow.
But all is not dead here: dogs scavenge for food traces,
while the rats play hopscotch on the
wrappers, food flotsam and jetsam and on excrement.
The life of the market can quickly turn to danger for the
foolish tourist here and there is always a blade
on every corner

Friends

Friends are for real
They don't beg, borrow or steal
They don't game or try to shame
They don't whisper or call you a name

Friends try – they really do
With real friends, there isn't only them, - there's you
Friends can click or they can slow burn
They stay the same and aren't pedantic or yearn

Its you, with all your weaknesses and peccadilloes
From your head right down to your toes
Achieve or not, succeed or fail
The friendship drive never veers form the trail

You may argue – of course you do – but it's all fun!
But in the end, they are always true
The laughs, the anecdotes and fun
When you die and it's all done they will be there for you

Friends are as rare as politicians are truthful
But through the hard times there's support to be done
And over the years you remain faithful
Work hard for your friends - be as one

Be selective.

July 2021
Dedicated to Zak Whitmill
I love you

T O D I E I N Y O U R A R M S

do not fret for me – my work is done
do not mourn my passing as I will always be with you
do not cry for what will not be in the future,
but rejoice at what has been in the past
do not forget me because I will never forget you
I love you

when the hurly burley's done
when the exams are passed
when the world is yours and your sons
remember how I squeezed and
hugged you every single day
I love you

these old eyes are filled with memories of us two
they are a movie of our life together
they saw you when you first came into this world
and now see you when I go
I love you

your greatness is my reward
your success is my legacy
your future is mine to savour
your life is mine to share
I love you

the memories wash over us
the intensity of our years together can only get stronger
our affection is etched in gold

the joy is beyond great
I love you

time is short
time to wonder at we two
time to change the script
time to move on
time to reflect on our lives together
I love you

as I look at you for the last time
as I gaze at your beautiful face
as I caress your head and squeeze your hand
As I smile with your smile
I love you

Twinned

Together again in angry peace they lay beside each other
The car crash of who was to blame will never be resolved
Twenty-five and twenty-nine: brothers in death

Schoolboys shouting and shivering in the cold comfort-less
classrooms
Drinking partners and playing darts
One drink too many – then no flights left

Empty girls and empty parents
Full graveyards, dead flowers, and deadened communities
The joined grief remembers them

Best mates, best nights out and best left in peace
Laughing, joking, working and dying
Together again after good times and bad judgements.

Fallen

I met an acquaintance the other day, around a corner and
unexpected
We recognized each other and talked for maybe 4 minutes
yet 40 years
A black woman, an old lover and work colleague – a taste
of youth from the past

We hugged and our cheeks lingered long and warm: the
smell of hair treatment and body butter
took me back a long way – to hot nights and tired days. Our
fingertips met as one carefully touches
live wires
She remembered my name and wistfully pierced my wide-
open eyes. Her soft looks and tones
rolled me around the bed and spat me out.

Nurses rooms, coloured homes of green, white and yellow
pictures melted into parquet floors,
high ceilings and wooden sash windows: single beds always
ready and always yearning for pleasure
A simpler time before the Hydra's head of materialism had
taken hold, of when politicians
could be trusted and you were what you had, not judged by
what you weren't....
A time when romance and love were real and not
manufactured.

Friendships and loves were formed on
the wards, where the washed-out décor led to coloured and
vibrant love making. The low wattage bulbs and low-level
lust melded as one: the mad within the

walls taught us to succour and value these trysts and to develop love for the inner person

'How are you' I tentatively asked, knowing how she used to be. She paused and said my
name.... 'Ah, Steve' said she...'we must have fallen'. My heart came up into my mouth, 'yes we did' I
muttered sheepishly. We parted, moist and sad and yet happy: wry smiles and searching memories:
Those days are gone, as have the nurse's homes and decaying hospital wards

We never met again, never shared, never gave, and never received.

Cloning for Love

For the preservation of love forever, it should be possible to
create endurance and the never-ending
Why should deep love and intense feeling be diminished or
terminated?
Only tragedy and time has the right to deliver such injustice
History is littered with broken hearts and unrequited love: it
bleeds with loss and torment

A lock of hair will freeze-frame the memory, relight the
visage and restore the feelings
A real-life presence part of you – forever: never to be taken
away, never to fade
As like words on parchment or lines inscribed on stone, the
feelings and love will outlast you – the
verse of love or tragedy splayed bare for all to see
The power of love will remain: the meaning sanctified

So, there is the choice: preserve forever or mourn forever or
Let to die and wither away
Let the science meet the love head-on and let the chemistry
meet the DNA and
Plan for immortality now
So that my son can be mine forever

The Graveyard

Amongst the intense quietness
There is a slow imperceptible swell going on
An Entish drawl, a drunken sway
The already decayed decay again, but they do not complain
as they lean and fall

The cloths of lichen try to hide the book of the dead....
Its liturgy drowning in the howls of tears
The stones and statues domino their dance while
the weeds suffocate them and new life challenges the old

The tragedy of unkemptness irks the observer, the mother,
the grandparent as
they shake their heads in dismay
Eyes are strained to lift words from the remains as fascination
brings them to life again
But old language and marks keep us from complete
understanding, sadly

The great, the ordinary – perhaps we too will lie here in the
graveyard – the last place
Loved and forgotten, remembered and lost: rotting and
eroded
The neglect from the living and the march of nature is finally
reclaimed by the glory of God
Until then, the dead wait and are at rest – their work is done
and their end is ours to behold

First Flush

I couldn't sleep, I couldn't think
I couldn't dare, I couldn't wink
My eyes were crazy and my mind confused
I didn't know how to proceed and felt bemused

My need stood proud and branched out long
My seed was waiting, my veins standing out strong
Drawn was I – propelled by the act
Not wanting fine words: just matter of fact

I looked at her paleness, her pertness and stance
Her virgin pink and her white tight pants
Her lips said welcome and her eyes said yes
I perceived such a vision of beauty – a visage in a dress

Her body, her form, her hair and her dress
Fine curves, mounds and waves of flesh
Past just wanting to admire, past just wanting to only desire
We collapsed breathless, awash with perspire

Her beauty had been transfixed, slayed and lost
She was my desire, my singularity of need
All as one in closeness body and mind
This moment, forever captured in time

Passing Out

God shines down directly on them
The blood of Britain – the pride of this land
Their set-piece service a dinner for glory or death
Their drilled faces and synchro meshed boots announce
them:
Polished, perfect, precision trained and formed

We ducks await the march by
and strain for a clear line of sight.
The deafening hot still air punctuated by the slap of weapon
on hip and glove;
The steely glance of every man and woman of them
They slowly wheel round and snake in front of the stand
As one: peacocks in brow, red. White, and shiny silver

They are in front of us now and our tears are in front of them:
we strain our eyes – just a glance
would do.
Our shutters have click as we strained on the edge of our
seats.
The transformation passes by and we hug each other,
overwhelmed
by the enormity of the moment
We try to see our little boy amongst the man that he is now -
I cry out his name

This England: this blood, this service to every one of us
This brand that draws fear and respect around the world
Our son is now this land's heritage.

His young laughs and tears honed metamorphosed into hardnosed order-giving and taking:
Yet somewhere, beneath, in moments of quietness, there will always be the fruit of our loins: the
product of love and joy
What was ours, however, is now there's.

Eaves Wood

A cacophony of colour everything in the valley
Resplendent shades punctuate the landscape; warm,
comforting, and mellow
Yet, sharp teeth are hidden and warn of danger from those
wander of the well-worn tracks
These crags have warm local affection and respect

Seeped in poetry and tinged with death
The incision hides it's past of hard labour and toil; words
and love
Reds, yellows, oranges, and browns layer over the sweat
and strain of history
and remind us of *her* summer dresses

Read the words of love and despair – forged from within the
bowels of the valley
Feel the traction of uncertainty and betrayal that drained
out from the lair
See the grave of her tragedy and ponder deeply at our loss
Reflect quietly on her legacy

But today, in autumn, the complimentary senses pay lip
service to tourists and wanderers:
nature arrays itself like a proud peacock in magnificence:
proud and vibrant
Eaves Wood is a heavenly kingdom of earth, for you to
respect and enjoy
How great are the works of God!

The Parsonage

The wind blew down and lifted latches
It snuffed out candles and rattled catches
Letters were lost and syllables ran out
Water scurried back up the water spout
Pages were scattered and men, women and children whisked away
Dogs howled and cats screeched – even the unholy preached
that Howarth day

Windows rattled and shutters flapped wide
The storm increased with nowhere to hide
Rain seeped under blinds and around doors
and the wind came cackling down from the moors
The dead covered their ears in the church grounds
and the vicar 's frock lifted, which made him frown
Forces of nature and God tested them that at that time
When the hours stopped and the clock refused to chime
Moans danced in the darkened corridors, moving up
and down between the floors

The girls held each other tight
on that terrible, terrible autumn night
Their words of comfort, not of prose or verse
amongst cries of alarm and curse
The fear and despair seen in their looks
Carefully transcribed into their books: preserved with ink and on page
The fury of the stormy rage

Black Crows

Pitch in pairs they descend
Circumspect and indifferent to all
Two of nothing they seem, on the garden's green base
Vulgar harbingers of scavenge and death to those who dare
to challenge them

These ancient negatives lord over their domain
With arrogance and naked ferocity
Holes in predation that are feared and fear nothing: their
blackness illustrates their dark intent
and the chartered approval of their type

See them like a tear in the sky as they space down towards
the ground
Guardians of our land and heritage and the scourge of dead
creatures
The black crows ink their history in this world, and are
always portrayed with fear in the next
Their harsh voices alarm all the living
Their devil eyes piercing all in their line of sight
Black crows: the presentation of the dark side, the
disagreeable side of birds…

Dark-Skinned Girl

I love you
I am possessed by your smouldering, smoky, smiling looks
You consume me and I'm going out of my mind
You have taken over my and.
I can't stand it

You flower me with your sexuality. You pawn your sex.
I do not have enough to want you enough
Your feminine attraction entrances me
You are part of me – I cannot think of anything without
thinking of you

It is 1986; we walk on the sea front and your womanhood
spills everywhere
I want this. I need you.
You are an icon of sensuality: a visage of desire
I'm losing my mind

We go to bed – heaven must be like this. A utopia of satiation.
You are not real: I am not in this space. I am married
But, I would give everything up for you. For this.
I am on autopilot and I cannot control it

It's 34 years later and I want you: I cannot let go.

Bucket Shitlist

You can't learn another language if you have dementia
You can't walk to Macu Picu if you have lost the use of your lower body
You can't learn to scuba dive in the Indian Ocean if you are confined to a wheelchair
You can't visit Easter Island if you are in intensive care

You won't write your life story if you have cerebral palsy
You won't fall in love if you are in a persistent vegetative state
You won't learn how to ballroom dance if you have had a major stroke
You won't stare at the wonders of the natural world is you cannot see

You will be far less fortunate that the rich retirees, who are lucky enough to enjoy their later life
You will be marginalised by the postcode lottery of care
You will be loved by those you have loved
You will be cared for by real wonderful people, who try to give some meaning and pleasure
to you in your twilight years

But most of all you will be you.

Lightning Source UK Ltd.
Milton Keynes UK
UKHW042337130222
398608UK00009B/55

9 781665 591737